D0323763

Koi for Home
and Garden
by
Glenn Y. Takeshita

Cover photos courtesy of Kodansha, Ltd.

ISBN 0-87666-754-X

Distributed in the U.S. by T.F.H. Publications, Inc., 211 West Sylvania Avenue, PO Box 427, Neptune, NJ 07753; in England by T.F.H. (Gt. Britain) Ltd., 13 Nutley Lane, Reigate, Surrey; in Canada to the pet trade by Rolf C. Hagen Ltd., 3225 Sartelon Street, Montreal 382, Quebec; in Canada to the book trade by H & L Pet Supplies, Inc., 27 Kingston Crescent, Kitchener, Ontario N28 2T6; in Southeast Asia by Y.W. Ong, 9 Lorong 36 Geylang, Singapore 14; in Australia and the South Pacific by Pet Imports Pty. Ltd., P.O. Box 149, Brookvale 2100, N.S.W. Australia; in South Africa by Valid Agencies, P.O. Box 51901, Randburg 2125 South Africa. Published by T.F.H. Publications, Inc., Ltd., the British Crown Colony of Hong Kong.

Acknowledgements

I would like to express my sincere thanks to each member of the Honolulu Goldfish and Carp Association for all the information and time so generously given; without the help of these people, this book could not have been written. To those who allowed me to photograph their koi to use as illustrations in the section showing koi varieties, I would like to extend an additional *Mahalo*, or thank you.

To those who are not in any way connected with the Honolulu Goldfish and Carp Association, but who gave up their valuable time, I extend my sincerest personal appreciation.

To Richard Matsui and Dr. Richard Boohar, who did most of the proofreading and made many constructive suggestions, many extra thanks.

A special thank you to Joseph Maeda, who did most of the photography, and to Ray Uyeda (1964 President of the Honolulu Goldfish and Carp Association), who provided much important information and help.

Mahalo again to all who contributed to making this book possible.

DEDICATION

This book is dedicated to the koi hobbyists of Hawaii.

PHOTOGRAPHS

Contents

Introduction

Since the end of World War II there has been in Hawaii a growing interest in the hobby of raising carp, or koi. This interest was triggered by importations from Japan of many new and colorful koi varieties, some of which were introduced for the first time. Because of them, the cultivation of koi has evolved through the years into a highly developed hobby with many scientific overtones.

Today in Hawaii, koi enthusiasts number in the hundreds, and many thousands of dollars are spent in importing and acquiring "superior" stock. The interest in koi has spread to the United States mainland, especially the West Coast, and there is now a national koi society in California.

This book is not to be viewed as a scientific work; it is more of a guide for the person who wants to know all of the basics and some of the fine points of keeping koi.

I hope that the information and observations cited will help readers to enjoy their koi to the fullest.

History

The koi, or fancy carp, is said to have had its origin in the Yama-koshi District of Niigata Prefecture in the northern part of the island of Honshu, Japan, during the Hei-an Period (794–1184 A.D.). It was only during the Momoyama Era (1582–1598 A.D.), however, that koi-raising became popular. Prior to this Era, only the rich and noble were privileged to keep the colorful koi. The first koi and their descendants of today are said to be offshoots of *Cyprinus carpio*, the common carp known to the Japanese as Ma-goi.

The first written reference to the cultivation of carp of any kind appeared in a Chinese manuscript written about 470 B.C. In Japanese literature the first documented reference to koi culture was a passage in a book dated 714 A.D. The carp was later described about 1758 A.D. by the famous naturalist Linnaeus, many years after it had been firmly established in Japan.

Long known for their skill in raising and perfecting many different types of pet animals, the Japanese have been especially successful in their work with koi and other carp-like species. Here an old-time Japanese street vendor displays his goldfish wares to a crowd of fascinated children.

Europeans as well as Orientals and Americans are interested in koi; the English, who have long been attracted to pool fish of all kinds, have done fine work in developing koi varieties. The koi shown here is an English fish.

The common carp, *Cyprinus carpio*, figures prominently in the ancestry of today's koi.

Goldfish are very closely related to koi, and no doubt both species share a common genealogy to a great extent.

A mixed population of
koi showing just a few
of the many koi color
varieties available.

The first Niigata koi were introduced to the public in 1914 during the Taisho Exposition. A total of 27 specimens were exhibited, the best seven of which were given to Crown Prince Hirohito as a gift from the officials of the Prefecture. It was then, during the Taisho Era (about 1912–1926 A.D.) through the Showa Era following, that many varieties of the colorful koi became firmly established.

Varieties like the Ki-Utsuri, Shiro-Utsuri, Kohaku and Sanshoku were developed during the Taisho Era, while colorful varieties like the Showa Sanshoku and Ginrin were developed during the Showa Era.

To the Japanese people, the koi symbolizes great strength and masculinity. And even today, the Fifth of May is still celebrated with the flying of paper and cloth kois to signify the birth of each son in the family.

Appropriately, the koi is called the "Warrior's Fish," but it also symbolizes "Love." Thus, the koi is of great emotional significance to the Japanese.

The exact date of introduction of the common river carp, *Cyprinus carpio*, into the Hawaiian Islands is unknown, but records show that it must have been before 1900. They were thought to have been first established in the reservoirs and streams on the islands of Maui and Kauai. It was also before 1900 that the common goldfish, *Carassius carassius*, or Funa, as we know them, was introduced.

The exact purpose for which the Ma-goi was first introduced into the Hawaiian Islands remains a mystery, for careful records were not kept in those days.

The "koi" of Hawaii are thought to be of Japanese lineage, but some authorities still feel that they are either a fancy variety of the common goldfish or a hybrid from the common goldfish and the carp.

If Hawaii's "koi" is indeed a hybrid between *Carassius carassius* and *Cyprinus carpio*, what about the sterility of male hybrid carp which Dr. Y. Matsui mentions in his paper, "Male Sterility of Hybrids of Carp and Crucian Carp or Goldfish"? This and many other questions pertaining to the parentage of Hawaii's koi lie unanswered. Until enough information to unravel this puzzle is collected, we will conform and consider koi to be just *different color varieties* of the common carp.

One big difference in the development of koi and the closely related gold-fish is that goldfish such as the bubble-eye shown here, have been bred extensively for distinctions in finnage and body shape, whereas koi varie-ties, represent primarily differentiations in color.

Shown in the foreground is one of the many lakes that lie at the foot of Mount Fujiyama in Japan; Mt. Fuji itself is in the background. The pen-like structure in the lake is used for fish culture.

Koi ponds are not strictly the preserve of people who live in areas having warm year-round climates. This pond, in which the fish are left outdoors during the winter even though the pond becomes completely covered with ice, is in New Jersey.

Pond Construction and Design

In Hawaii, with its many different types of gardens prepared by its cosmopolitan population, various sizes and shapes of ponds are seen. Some of them lack, and others have, the design for good maintenance for koi raising. But whether the garden is in Hawaii or Hoboken, not every garden pond makes a good koi pond. In order for a pond to be of maximum utility in the maintenance of koi, its design should include the following elements:

1. It should have a *minimum* water depth of 16 to 20 inches. (The colder the winters experienced in the area, the deeper the pond needs to be.)
2. The sides should be raised at least 4 inches or higher above the ground level to prevent flooding or overflowing during a heavy rainstorm.

Calternifolius variegatus, the umbrella plant, is a favorite landscape plant among pool owners.

Beautifully colorful water lilies heighten the attractiveness of any koi pool in which they are used.

3. There should be at least one central area with a water depth of $2\frac{1}{2}$ feet.
4. Some method of aeration of the pond water should be provided.
5. Some method of filtering the water *must* be provided.
6. The pond floor should be sloped toward the deeper central area to facilitate removal of waste.
7. A simulated water current should be provided for exercising the koi and for aiding in concentrating the koi's waste in the designated deep central area.
8. A partially shaded area should be provided for the koi as a retreat from the more sunny and exposed area.
9. Pond plants like the water lily, shobu, etc., should be provided but they are not strictly necessary.

The trend today is toward the building of rectangular tile ponds instead of the more expensive "moss rock" ponds, although the more expensive moss rock ponds can also be seen quite frequently. This type of pond is generally blended into an Oriental landscaping scheme to create a feeling of peace and serenity.

Koi pond setup showing ornamental aquatic plants like the Shobu and water lily, plus a good koi collection. The owner of the koi pond and its fish is Mr. Herbert T. Hayashi.

A moss rock-tile outdoor pool housing koi; this pond is at the Pineapple Research Institute of Hawaii.

Closeup of the waterfall area of a moss rock type pond.

The flowering rush, *Butomus umbellatus,* is a hardy plant that does well in koi pools and adds a highly decorative touch.

A moss rock type pond utilizing traditional Oriental landscaping scheme; this pool is situated at the Pagoda Floating Restaurant in Hawaii.

Aquatic plants play a very important role in the koi pool through their capacity for shading the water from the direct rays of the sun, thereby helping to control the proliferation of algae while regulating the temperature of the water.

A moss rock-tile pond at the East-West Center of the University of Hawaii.

Tile koi pond owned by Stanley G. Maeshiro of Hawaii.

To calculate the volume of a pond, multiply the width by the length by the height of the water level in the pond. This will give you the volume in either cubic feet or cubic inches. If your answer is in cubic feet, multiply the figure obtained by 7.5 gals./cu.ft. to give you the volume in gallons (U.S.). If the result is in cubic inches, divide your answer by 1728, to get the answer in cubic feet; then multiply the number of cubic feet by 7.5 gals. to get your volume in gallons (U.S.).

Conversion factor: 1 cubic foot = 7.5 gallons (U.S.).

Examples :

1. Given: Dimensions of pond: Length = 10 feet.
   - Width = 3 feet.
   - Height = 1 feet (water level).

   Volume of pond = 10 ft. × 3 ft. × 1 ft. = 30 cu. ft.

   Therefore: Volume of pond = 30 cu. ft. × 7.5 gals./cu. ft. = 225 gals.

2. Given: Dimensions of pond: Length = 120 inches.
   *1 cu. ft. = 1728 cu. in. Width = 36 inches.
   - Height = 12 inches.

   Volume of pond (in cu. in.) = 120 in. × 36 in. × 12 in. = 51,840 cu. in.

   Volume of pond (in cu. ft.) = 51840 ÷ 1728 = 30 cu. ft.

   Therefore: Volume of pond (in gals. U.S.) = 30 cu. ft. × 7.5 gals./cu. ft. = 225 gals.

The cattail, genus *Typha,* is a tall pool-side plant that adds interest and beauty to the koi pond.

Various views of the show floor at the first All-Japan
koi show.

Care and Feeding

Koi are hardy, adaptable fish that don't make too many demands on their owners regarding the type of water they'll live in and the type of food they'll eat. They are especially adaptable as regards temperature requirements, doing best while maintained at a temperature level of 65 to 70° but living safely in waters ranging from 40 to 95°. In Hawaii, the air temperature seldom goes below 60 or above 90°, so the water in the koi ponds remains fairly constant at between 74 and 78°. In other places, koi have been known to have survived in ponds that regularly become frozen over to a depth of several inches during the winter and in ponds in which the temperature rises to 112° in summer. Therefore the problem of maintaining a livable temperature for koi lies not so much in providing a narrow optimum range as in making sure that the temperature does not fluctuate widely within a short period of time. One of the advantages of having a large pond, by the way, is that temperature fluctuations occur less rapidly in a large pond than in a small one.

The ideal environmental conditions for the koi are as follows:

1. Water temperature: 65–70° F. In Hawaii kept at 74–78° F.
   - (*a*) Survival temperature range: 30° F.–112° F.
   - (*b*) Safe temperature range: 40° F.–95° F.
   - *Note:* Large fluctuations of water temperature should be avoided at all times to prevent the koi from getting chilled. (Optimum temperature difference tolerance is 40° F.).

2. The water should be slightly on the alkaline side; a pH reading of 7.0 to 7.5 is ideal. Actually, koi are able to tolerate a large range of pH without difficulty, provided the water does not change in character abruptly. To be on the safe side, make periodic checks with one of the inexpensive pH kits available.

3. Koi are fairly heavy users of oxygen, so their water should contain as much dissolved oxygen as possible. An ideal dissolved oxygen concentration would be 8 parts per million. Dissolved oxygen (D.O.) concentrations of less than 2 ppm could easily be fatal. Since the D.O. level in pond water drops appreciably at night, artificial aeration of the water should be provided at night. Any method of agitating the surface of the water tends to aerate the water, but the most reliable method, and no doubt the most satisfactory in the long run, is to use one of the specially designed

Kits for measuring the pH of water are inexpensive and very easy to use; they represent a very sensible investment.

pond pumps that are on the market. They can be used to both aerate and filter the water.

Koi use more oxygen when the temperature of the water is high than when it is low, and this is one reason why it is dangerous to let the koi pool become too warm.

4. Water to be used in the koi pond should be treated to remove chlorine before fish are introduced. Underground waters and rain water are usually undesirable unless they have been treated, for the former is low in dissolved oxygen and the latter contains relatively high concentrations of harmful substances.

Under ideal environmental conditions, the life span of the koi is between 10 and 20 years, during which time it attains a length of 18 to 30 inches.

In nature the koi avoids churning, swift waters like rapids and instead seeks out still waters found in large ponds. But in an enclosed artificial system like our man-made ponds, a moderate to strong current in the water at the bottom of the pond is a good thing to have, for it exercises the koi and in that way stimulates a better appetite, producing a bigger and stronger fish.

第一回　全日本総合錦鯉品評会

These are the trophies that were awarded to winners in the different classes at the first All-Japan koi show held in late 1968.

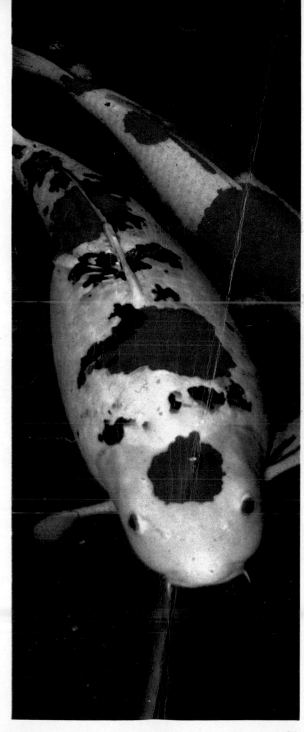

This Taisho
Sanke was the
Grand Champion
of the first All-
Japan koi show
held in Tokyo
in 1968.

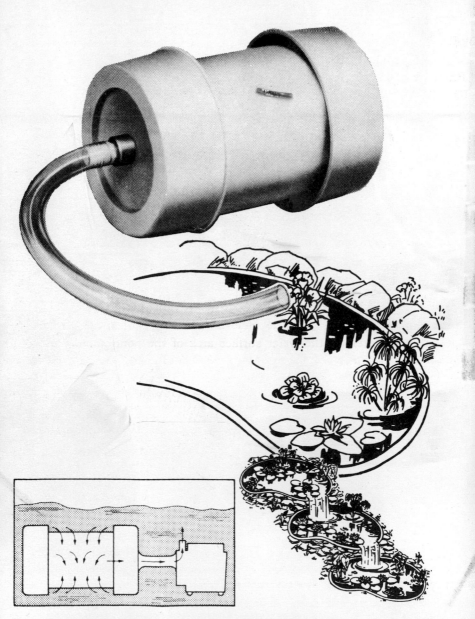

Filters designed specifically for use in ponds are very useful in maintaining water quality. The unit shown is connected to a water pump that circulates water through the filter, trapping the dirt in a reusable foam sleeve. Courtesy Eugene G. Danner Co.

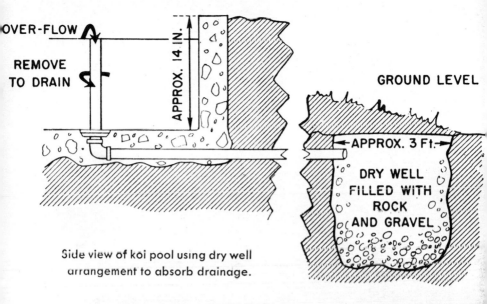

OVER-FLOW

REMOVE
TO DRAIN

APPROX. 14 IN.

GROUND LEVEL

←APPROX. 3 Ft.→

DRY WELL
FILLED WITH
ROCK
AND GRAVEL

Side view of koi pool using dry well
arrangement to absorb drainage.

Since koi are large fishes, they require a great deal of dissolved oxygen; therefore, the water surface area of the pond should be as great as possible. The depth of the water should be low if the pond is not mechanically aerated, because the oxygen which enters at the surface of the water can be better distributed to the bottom reaches of the pond.

Artificial aeration is not a "must" if you have a large water surface and only a few koi, but aeration is recommended if this condition cannot be obtained.

FILTRATION

Filtration of the water is very important. Many koi raisers do not filter their water, thinking that filters for ponds are "inefficient." The author feels that a modified standard gravity slow sand filter should work quite well. This filter may be a little expensive initially but should save many dollars and plenty of hard work as the years go by. One aquarium products manufacturer offers an undergravel pool filter designed specifically to filter outdoor fish pools, and this filter does an excellent job.

The size of the sand filter will depend on the rate (gals./min.) at which your recirculating pump can operate. The ideal rate at which the sand filter can work efficiently is 0.2 gals./ft.^{2}/min. (This is the average).

A mixed population of
koi showing good
specimens of many
color varieties.

This frontal view of two
koi shows the head
structure and
multicolored pectoral
fins.

Example for calculation of the surface dimensions of the sand filter:
Given: Rate of recirculating pump = 10 gals./min.
        Ideal rate for filtration = 0.2 gals./ft.^{2}/min.
        X = Surface area of sand filter.
Formula:
Surface area of sand filter = Rate of recirculating pump ÷
                                    Ideal rate for filtration
Therefore:
X = 10 gals./min. ÷   = 50 ft.^{2} or filter has to have a surface
     0.2 gals./min. ft.^{2} area of approx. 7 ft. × 7 ft.

The function of a burlap bag at the pre-filtration effluent is to remove any large suspended material in the water and prevent splashing, and the job of the sand filter is to remove all the other smaller suspended material that the burlap bag did not filter out. Because of the burlap bag the period of efficiency of the sand filter is extended. The burlap bag should be removed and cleaned at least once a week to insure good pre-filtration. Other types of bags may be substituted if burlap bags are not available, providing that they are made of a very strong porous material capable of being in the water for a long time.

For the sand layer in the filter, beach sand of uniform size is recommended. If beach sand containing a great deal of carbonate material is used, the water in the pond will increase in hardness and pH over a period of time. But this increase is not of the magnitude to create any harmful effects on the koi.

Since the sand filter will not filter out any dissolved material, it is recommended that part of the water in the pond be changed at least once a week.

Since there is a tendency for scum formation at the water surface, water should be added to the pond periodically to remove this scum by overflowing. Efficiency of the water filtration will depend on the scum scavenging setup (on the pond bottom as well as the water surface) and the capacity of the recirculating pump.

The steps in cleaning the sand filter are as follows:
1. Stop recirculating pump.
2. Let all the water in the pre-filtration box and sand filter drain out.
3. Remove drain from pre-filtration box. Then hose down and scrub the box. Also hose down the root systems of the water hyacinths thoroughly. Replace drain plug.

4. In the sand filter remove at least $\frac{1}{2}$ inch of sand from its surface layer. Throw this sand away.
5. Start the recirculating pump again to refill the pre-filtration box and sand filter with water.

The interval between cleaning the filter should be left up to the individual hobbyist, for the amount of filtration needed will vary with each pond.

By following these simple rules, efficient and economical filtration of the pond water can be obtained.

It must be understood that this is just one of the many efficient filtration setups for ponds. But it is not the only one which will give efficient results. Other systems are just as good and efficient and are being utilized by many large fish hatcheries and farms all over the world.

FEEDING

Feeding koi is not a very difficult task, for most koi will accept any fresh or dried prepared foods. Also, both animal and vegetable foods are eaten eagerly. But the trick to success in feeding is to provide them with a *nutritious, well balanced diet.*

Most koi raisers in Hawaii use a basic diet of dry prepared trout meal supplemented by other foods such as (1) washed fresh earthworms, (2) tubifex worms, (3) insect larvae and pupae, (4) naked

Many of the flake foods—including those designed as conditioners and color enhancers—produced for feeding to tropical fishes are equally suitable for use with koi, and they provide variety in the diet.

Holding and rearing ponds for koi such as those shown here are a fairly common sight in many Japanese towns.

Koi holding ponds situated in a mountain lake.

These holding crates are used for separating various types of koi.

This fish culturist is netting young koi from a rearing pond.

This photograph shows an actual Japanese koi auction. Prospective buyers have a chance to inspect the koi at close range.

shellfish, (5) toasted silk worms, (6) special koi pellets from Japan, (7) chopped lettuce, cabbage, carrots, and watercress, and (8) crushed crayfish, crab, or shrimp. Diet is greatly varied and modified depending on the individual hobbyist.

The basic rule to remember in feeding is to give the fish a well balanced diet, not feeding too much of any one food. Green vegetables are definitely essential. Greens should be given at least two times a week or more often if possible.

Most koi fanciers in Hawaii feed their fishes twice a day—once in the morning and once at early evening. The heaviest feeding is generally in the evening.

Fresh water is piped into the pond just previous to the heaviest feeding each day. This procedure will generally increase the fish's appetite and is practiced by many of the koi fanciers with good results. Feedings should be liberal but not excessive.

Feeding of color foods has just in the past few years crept into the koi picture. but since dependable data are still very scarce, great strides in this phase of feeding are yet to come. Vital stains and carotinoid derivatives have been tried for color intensification with marginal success.

If one wishes to enjoy the pleasure of watching the Koi when feeding, bread-like feed which will float on the water should be prepared having the following composition:

Fish powder, fish meat	25%
Pupa powder	25%
Rice cake, flour, soybean cake	30%
Potatoes	10%
Vegetables	9%
Table salt	1%

When the water temperature is below 68° F., the proportion of the vegetable components should be increased. Above 80° F., the proportion of animal components should be increased.

During the summer months, it is very desirable for the koi to fast for a period of 10 days. But, if at any time the water temperature falls below 60° F., the koi should be fed some submersible food once a month or not at all.

When a new stock of koi is received, they should be kept on one third the normal diet for the first 10 days.

If the water temperature is below 70° F., give the koi easily digestible food every other day.

Pelletized foods, which are available in the form of both floating pellets and sinking pellets, are one of the most convenient foods for use in feeding pond-housed fishes.

A group of koi showing
good specimens of
Asagi, Shiro-muji, Shiro
Bekko, Kohaku, Showa-
Sanke, Taisho-Sanke,
and Hi-Utsuri.

Mixed koi population
that includes good
representatives of
Kohaku, Shiro Utsuri,
Hi-Utsuri, Showa-
Sanke, and Shusui.

In areas where seasonal changes are pronounced (as in Japan), the recommended feeding schedule is as follows:

Feed koi three times a day: at 9 A.M., noon, and 4 P.M. The amount of feed given should be as much as the koi can consume completely in ten minutes. During spring and fall, two meals are recommended, one at 10 A.M. and one at 3 P.M. In winter, do not feed as long as the water temperature remains below 41° F. At temperatures above 95° F. do not feed the koi at all.

FEEDING METHODS AND TRAINING

To feed the koi from the edge of the pond, natural foods should be given over a long period. In approaching the pond, movements should be quiet and slow. Kneeling at the edge of the pond and stretching out of the hand for feeding should be executed also with slow, deliberate movements. The same precaution should be followed when leaving the pond.

If these basic steps are followed, the koi will soon respond to your clapping of hands, splashing of the water or your footsteps to seek the food you bring them.

In feeding the koi, it is a very good practice to place the food in the same spot at each feeding. If you do this, you may feed your koi from two to ten times a day providing that you feed them so that they are only half satisfied. This feeding procedure should be followed until your koi are completely trained.

The following are training practices followed by Japanese fanciers. Basically, both methods are very similar and can be modified to suit your personal taste.

JAPANESE TRAINING METHODS*

First day—After releasing the koi into the pond, reduce the rate of fresh water inflow in order to keep the pond water as undisturbed as possible.

Second day—Approach the pond with muffled footsteps so as not to surprise the koi. Approach the pond in the afternoon and clap your hands several times. Just as the first day, do not feed them.

Third day—Splash the water with your hands to attract their attention. No food should be given.

Fourth day and thereafter—Repeat the third day's pattern until the koi come up close to the water's surface and bob up and down looking for food.

*Hirooka, Hyohei: *The Care and Training of Koi*—March 30, 1964.

42

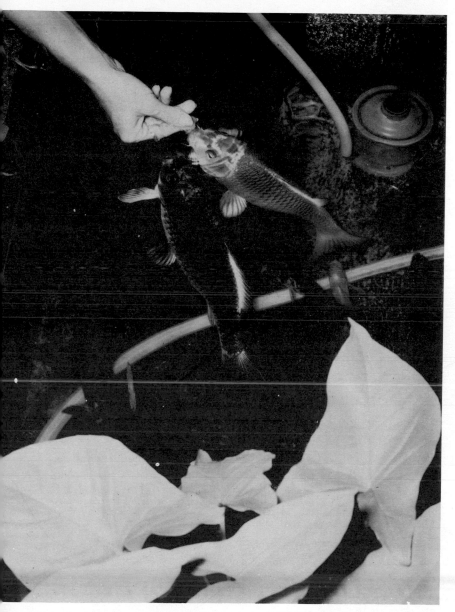

One of the biggest delights of owning a koi pool comes from having the fish respond by coming to take food from their owner's hands at feeding time.

Pelleted foods designed for use with pool fishes generally contain the correct proportion of vegetable material, an important consideration with fishes of the carp family such as koi.

Feeding time at the Pagoda Floating Restaurant in Honolulu, Hawaii. The koi are fed at 8 a.m., noontime, and 6 p.m. daily. At feeding time they are summoned to the feeding area by the ringing of a bell. These koi are owned by Herbert T. Ayashi.

Throw grass cuttings or other similar material out onto the water. If the koi nibble at them, give them food. If they eat the food completely, add more. It is essential, however, to stop feeding them before they become gorged. With respect to daily meals, it is advisable to rally and feed them in several installments so that they may eat their food in a short period of time. After this has become an established pattern, you can be sure that they will gather around whenever you clap your hands and will even take bread from your hand.

Breeding

The breeding of Hawaii's koi is undertaken in spring and early summer through fall; in areas having a less clement climate than Hawaii, the breeding season is much shorter.

Sexing of the breeder koi is accomplished by looking for the following anatomical features in the adults:

Female: When viewed from above, the body is very broad and rounded from the gill plate area to three-quarters of an inch past the dorsal fin. The pectoral fins are blunt and rounded and the gill area is smooth during breeding season. The breeding female should be $1\frac{1}{2}$ to 2 years or older.

Male: The pectoral fins protrude, and their first rays are lumpy and pointed. The body shape is very slender from the gill plate on down. During the mating season the gill plate area becomes very rough. The breeding male should be over 3 years old.

Breeding quarters should be small ponds (6 ft. × 8 ft.) with about 1 to $1\frac{1}{2}$ feet of water. Place many water hyacinths with large root systems in these ponds to act as spawning medium. In Japan, willow roots are used instead of water hyacinths as spawning medium. Sphagnum moss placed in screen baskets may also be used. The eggs are sprayed on these root systems during the height of spawning.

Hawaii's breeders generally use one female and two males, but some breeders use more males to insure better fertilization of the eggs.

For quality progeny, adults of the same strain should be bred.

The breeding pond should be very clean and devoid of algae. Tap water is used in the breeding pond; all feeding is stopped during breeding.

The breeder koi are placed in the breeding ponds during the day.

Male koi chase the female trying to drive her toward the spawning medium (in this case, water lettuce, *Pistia stratiotes*). This spawning took place at about eight o'clock in the morning.

After a few hours or few days of active courtship (continued chasing of the female by the males) within the breeding quarters, the eggs will be laid during the early morning hours (any time from 12 midnight to 6 A.M.). Dropping of the water temperature artificially by placing ice cubes into the water may help to induce spawning.

The breeder koi should be removed from the breeding pond as soon as they have finished spawning, or they will eat the eggs.

If spawning has not occurred after one week, the breeders should be placed back in their community pond to be rested. After two weeks of conditioning, the breeding can again be attempted.

Many koi raisers believe that the shape of the male determines vitality and virility, the more streamlined and firmly built being the more virile and active.

The number of eggs laid per female generally runs from about 100,000 to 750,000, depending on the size and condition of the female. The eggs are small—about 0.33 millimeters in diameter and of a transparent to greenish tinge.

Both koi are Kohaku.

At center of photo,
Kin-ki-utsuri koi.

At center, Asagi.

At center, Ohgon koi.

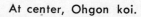

Aka-muji (Beni-goi). This specimen is rare in that it possesses a golden overcast over its entire body; this feature is highly cherished.

This Aka-muji (Beni-goi) is an excellent specimen of its color variety, since it possesses an intensified red body color. It also lacks any black tick marking on its body, making it a very fine show specimen.

These are brine shrimp nauplii, newly hatched young of the marine crustacean *Artemia salina;* brine shrimp nauplii are a very good food for koi fry.

At a temperature between 80° and 83° F., the eggs hatch in three days, and the fry should be free-swimming about a week after they have hatched out.

The fry are comparatively large, so rearing them on a standard brine shrimp diet presents no problems. The fry will grow at a tremendous rate if provided with an adequate amount of food. A slow-down in the young koi's growth rate can be seen after they have attained a length of between one and two inches. The reason for this slowing down is not known. But after a few months under ideal conditions, the koi will again commence growing at a steady rate until they reach maturity. Hawaii's koi attain maturity at an average of $1\frac{1}{2}$ to 4 years, but there may be exceptions to the rule.

The young koi should be separated by color at the age of one month, to facilitate selection of superior individuals.

Breeders in Hawaii feel that the rate of growth should be slow on patterned koi if they are to hold their color. The growth rate of the solid-colored progeny is not as critical, for here loss of color is not very marked and important.

Most Hawaiian koi enthusiasts agree that show specimens should not be bred at all, for they say that a loss of color occurs, probably due to the hardships on bodily metabolism and physiology during spawning.

Koi Varieties

Koi come in as many colors as the rainbow which so often graces the sky over Hawaii. Other wonderful attributes of the lovely koi are its many varied shapes and color patterns.

In Hawaii, the *"exactness of patterns,"* the *"intensity of color,"* and the *"soundness of conformation"* are forever sought after. It is the combination of these attributes which determine the value of the koi.

The many color varieties of koi are generally divided into five major groups by Japanese hobbyists. The groups are: (1) Hikali Mono group (bright); (2) Doitsu group (German; large-scaled or scaleless); (3) Taisho group (basic color either white or red); (4) Showa group (basic color black); and (5) Asagi group (basic color blue).

This European mirror carp, a variety of *Cyprinus carpio*, exhibits the large scales characteristic of the Doitsu type of koi. Older specimens of both carp and Doitsu koi often lose the scales along the sides through abrasion with objects in water.

Four males in close pursuit of the lone female during the spawning act.

A number of aquatic pests of all types, usually the juvenile and adult stages of various aquatic insects, prey on baby koi. Certain dangerous insect larvae like the larva of the dragonfly shown here should be eliminated from the breeding pool.

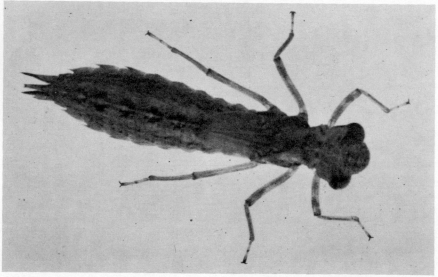

The female koi has been driven almost completely out of the water by the males during the height of the spawning act.

Two males and the ripe female are in position near the water lettuce just prior to the actual spawning procedure.

Kokucho-Shusui, top view.

Kokucho-Shusui, side view.

In Hawaii, koi are judged in 21 groups instead of the five basic groups used in Japan.

Although all color varieties can be placed somewhere in the five basic groups, Hawaiian hobbyists have adopted the 21-class judging scheme to avoid confusion arising from overlapping that might occur if only five groups were used.

In judging, conformation counts 50%, exactness of patterns counts 25%, and intensity of color counts 25%. In monochromatic koi, the intensity of color is of secondary importance to conformation, for here the pattern is not considered or is of minor importance. All koi, except the Shusui, are judged by conformation, back pattern, and color. In the Shusui, the intensity of the red or orange color covering the belly portion is of the greatest importance. The coloration of the belly portion of all other color varieties of koi is not considered.

It is the purpose of the following photographs and descriptions to present the standards which the koi fanciers of Hawaii follow.

In this section, emphasis will be placed on names, descriptions, and hints for selection, supplemented by diagrams where possible. The ultimate goal is to provide enough information about selection to enable the hobbyist to select above average koi for his own collection.

Considering the great variety of koi already available and the even greater number currently being developed, it is impossible to provide information on every known variety, so this book concentrates on the most important varieties known to the author, with emphasis on those koi that are significant among Hawaiian hobbyists.

KOHAKU
Kohaku (red and white) or "Sarasa" (Chintz)

A. Description: The main color is white, with red accents. Kohaku koi may be normally scaled or Doitsu. This color variety is thought to be the greatest in number today.

B. Popular types of Kohaku are as follows:

1. *Tancho*—All white except for a red triangle on the head.
2. *Hinomaru-Tancho*—All white except for the red on the head; the red area on the head should be circular in shape.
3. *Date-musume*—Main color is white, with red head, red on the back by the dorsal fin, and red on the nape of the tail, evenly spaced.

Water lettuce, *Pistia stratiotes,* one of the plants used to serve for receipt of the eggs of spawning koi. Illustration by Mirko Vosatka.

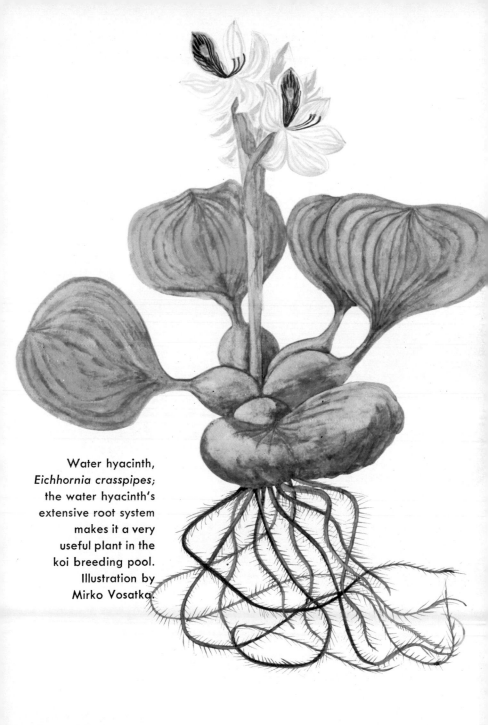

Water hyacinth,
Eichhornia crasspipes;
the water hyacinth's
extensive root system
makes it a very
useful plant in the
koi breeding pool.
Illustration by
Mirko Vosatka.

4. *Sakura*—Main color is white, with circular red accents symbolizing cherry blossoms.
C. Selection hints:
1. Red should be as intense as possible.
2. Red area should have a definite design or pattern.
3. The red area should not extend to the belly area but instead be localized in the back or dorsal area. The red on the head should remain preferably above the eye level.
4. The white background should be milk white, not pinkish white.

HARE-WAKE DOITSU OHGON
"Doitsu" (mirror carp, king carp, leather carp, German carp, or Speigel carp)

A. Discussion: This is a hybrid of the German and the Japanese fancy carp. This variety was first produced about 1904 by a Mr. Akiyama. The first developed specimen of this type was the Shusui. Mr. Akiyama developed the Shusui by crossing the mirror carp of Germany with the Japanese Narumi Asagi.

The original mirror carp (leather carp) were just "sports" of the common river carp (*Cyprinus carpio*) which became established in the waters in Europe. In the wild state, the specimens which had one row of large scales on the back and on the lateral line were called saddle carps. As these carp aged, the large scales dropped off because of continuous scraping against objects during feeding. The specimens which became scaleless were then called leather carps. As for the pond-raised variety, the large scales may remain intact for the entire life span of the carp.

It was from these original mirror or leather carps of Germany that Mr. Akiyama developed the first specimens of the Japanese Doitsu-type koi.

Today, any koi with the large scales or the scaleless body are all lumped together and given the general name of Doitsu. When koi fanciers use the term "Doitsu," they are talking about a koi with anatomical characteristics of the original mirror or leather carps of Germany. Translated, *Doitsu* in Japanese means "German," and therein lies the association of the large scaled and scaleless characteristics of the first imported carps from Germany with the word "Doitsu."

B. Description: Doitsu-type koi may be fully scaled with extra large scales or semi-scaled with large scales running along the top and middle of the body, parallel with the tail; they may also be scaleless. All color varieties of koi may be Doitsu (either with the extra large scales or scaleless, or a combination of both of these characteristics). The word "Doitsu" is used in front of the name of the specific color variety. Examples: Doitsu-Sanke ; Doitsu-Kohaku.

C. Selection hints:

1. If semi-scaled with large scales on the back and at the lateral line, the large scales should be as uniform as possible with no break at all.

2. If scaleless, there should not be any scales at all if possible.

KOKUCHO-SHUSUI

Shusui (autumnal water)

A. Discussion: This variety is named after its developer, Mr. Akiyama. Most koi fanciers literally translate the Japanese word "*Shusui*" as autumnal water. But what koi fanciers do not know is that the Japanese character for "*Shu*" is the same as for "*Aki*," which means autumn. "*Aki*" is actually taken from Mr. Akiyama's name to honor him in the development of this variety.

B. Description: Blue or gray top half with all finnage, cheeks, and undersides red or orange. In color, the Shusui is exactly like the Asagi, but the Shusui is only of the Doitsu type. The blue on top and the red underneath suggests autumn in Japan, when the azure blue sky outlines the red maple (*Momiji*) leaves on the ground.

C. Selection hints:

1. The back of the koi should be "clean," without any spotting by other colors.

2. The red or orange color of the underside should be evenly distributed and as dark and intense as possible.

3. In semi-scaled specimens, hints in the Doitsu section also apply here.

4. Base color should be as pure and rich as possible.

TAISHO-SANKE

Taisho-Sanke (Taisho-Sanshoku; Taisho-Tricolor)

A. Discussion: This tricolored variety was created in the Taisho Era

The triangular red marking on the head of this basically all-white koi shows it to be a Tancho variety of Kohaku koi.

(1917) of Japanese history. Since the colors are so delicately patterned, it is not easy to produce them. Koi of this variety are said to be very slow-growing.

B. Description: Main color is white, with accents of red and black.
C. Selection hints:
    1. The three colors should be pure and the pattern exact, with no overlap or masking of the colors at the edges of the pattern. A very good specimen is highly priced and prized.

This Kohaku koi would be considered to be a good specimen if it weren't for the red spot below its eye on the cheek area.

This Hare-Wake Doitsu Ohgon incorporates the large-scale pattern introduced into koi stocks by crossings with domesticated strains of the common river carp.

2. Specimens under 6 inches would be almost impossible to use for show purposes, for the exactness of pattern and intensity of color develops with age. At a very young age, this variety is predominately gray or black in color, making selection of show specimens much more difficult.

SHOWA-SANKE

Showa-Sanke (Showa-Tricolor; Showa-Sanshoku)

A. Description: Tricolored; the main color is black, with accents of red and white. Many experts feel that this color variety, once established, will undergo few further changes in color and pattern. Color fading is very unusual. This variety is said to have been developed in the Showa Era of Japanese history.

B. Selection hints:

1. The red and white minor colors should be evenly distributed on the black background.
2. The black color should extend vertically from the back to the belly area.
3. The three colors should be very dark and intense. The white color should be a milk white and not a pinkish-white.

SHIRO UTSURI

Shiro-utsuri (white reflection)

A. Description: A duochromatic (black and white) koi, the main color is black, with accents of white. Shiro-utsuri koi are thought to have been developed by crossing the Shiro-Bekko with the Ki-utsuri. Their white spots may sometimes come and go.

B. Selection hints:
1. As in the Showa, the black color is dominant, and the white should be milk white and evenly distributed.
2. Pattern should be exact with clean cut edges. The white spots or areas should be fairly large but not speckled.

HI-UTSURI

Ki-utsuri (yellow reflection) and Hi-utsuri (scarlet reflection)

A. Description:
1. *Ki-utsuri*—Main color is black, with accents of yellow.
2. *Hi-utsuri*—Main color is black, with accents of red or orange.

In many specimens of these varieties, the fins may also be streaked with yellow, red, or orange.

Hi-utsuri koi, female.

The Ki-utsuri was developed by crossing the Magoi with the Ki-bekko.

The Hi-utsuri was developed by crossing the Ki-utsuri with the Aka-bekko.

B. Selection hints:
1. Like the Shiro-utsuri, the black base color should be pure and dark. The pattern created by the yellow, red, or orange accents should be definite; it should not blend at the edges of the pattern.
2. The yellow, red, or orange areas should be pure and devoid of any black specks, if possible.
3. The yellow, red, or orange color may run into the dorsal, caudal, or pectoral fins.

KIN-KI-UTSURI

Kin-showa-sanke and Kin Ki-utsuri (Kin-showa-sanshoku)

A. Description:
1. *Kin-showa-sanke*—Main color is black, with accents of white and red. The red portion is generally metallic orange instead of deep red, while the whole body is metallic in color.
2. *Kin ki-utsuri*—Main color is black, with accents of yellow and orange, the whole body of the koi being highly metallic in color. The yellow and orange areas are very highly metallic gold.

B. Selection hints:
1. For the two above-mentioned varieties, the most highly metallic colored individuals should be selected at all times.
2. Definite pattern and intensity of color are other attributes to consider during selection.

ORANGE OHGON

Orange or Yellow Ohgon=(Beni-Ohgon, Oranji-Ohgon; Yamabuki Ohgon)

A. Description: All members of this Ohgon variety are highly metallic kois. They may be the orange, yellow, silver, white, red, gold, etc., types.

The Ohgon varieties are metallic throughout the body, with strong metallic accents on the top side (on dorsal line and fins) and also in the head area (the crown of the head). *Ohgon* means "golden yellow" in Japanese.

Traditional Japanese koi pond
housing a mixed population of
koi.

Taisho-Sanke

Ai-goromo

Showa-Sanke

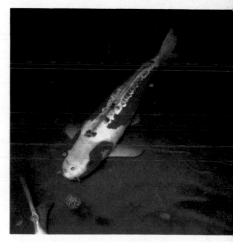

Shusui

Orange Ohgon, male; all of the Ohgon koi should be as metallic in sheen as possible.

According to Mr. Buhei Hoshida (an authority on the Ohgon variety), the Ohgon's color brilliance is said to be intensified when the water temperature is about 64° F. and below. It is during October to April that the color of the Ohgon variety becomes most spectacular.

The Ohgon variety was developed by a poor farmer named Sawata Aoki and his son over a period of 30 years. This variety was first introduced to the public in 1946.

B. Types of Ohgon:
   1. *Orange-Ohgon (Beni-Ohgon)*—Red or orange, but highly metallic throughout the entire body.
   3. *Yellow-Ohgon (Yamabuki-Ohgon)*—Yellow, but highly metallic throughout the entire body.

C. Selection hints:
   1. For both the Orange and Yellow Ohgon the most important characteristic is the metallic sheen; the more highly metallic, the better.
   2. The second point to consider is the purity and intensity of base color and the blending of the color shades and overtones.

SHIRO-MUJI

Muji Family

A. Description: Monochromatic; solid or plain in color.

B. Types of the Muji family:
1. *Aka-muji*—All red.
2. *Shiro-muji*—All white (with or without red eyes).
3. *Ki-goi*—All yellow (with or without red eyes).
4. *Cha-goi*—Light reddish-brown (color of tea).
5. *Ma-goi*—Common brown river type.
6. *Karasu*—All black (like the black of a crow).

C. Selection hints:
1. All Muji should have only one color, but clear or white-finned individuals are acceptable.
2. The main color should not have any specks or blemishes of any other color.
3. It is very common to have highly metallic specks of gold or silver (kin or gin) on the scales of these varieties.
4. The Muji type specimens can come from any of the color varieties, but it is almost impossible to find a perfect show specimen.

SHIRO-BEKKO

Aka-Bekko, Ki-Bekko, or Shiro-Bekko (red, yellow or white tortoise-shell)

A. Description: Here the pattern of the koi is said to resemble closely the pattern found on the shell of the tortoise.

B. Types of Bekko:
1. *Aka-Bekko*—Main color is red, with accents of black.
2. *Shiro-Bekko*—Main color is white, with accents of black.
3. *Ki-Bekko*—Main color is yellow, with accents of black.

C. Selection hints:
1. The black areas should be medium to large blotches, with not many small specks on the back-ground color.
2. Purity, clarity, and intensity of the background and accent color are important.
3. Symmetry of design is very important.
4. Clear or white fins are acceptable.

Goshiki

Shusui koi; note
the large scales
that differentiate
the Shusui from
the Asagi, which
has the same type
of coloration.

Matsuba Ohgon koi.

The color pattern of the tricolor Taisho Sanke should be crisp and clear.

This is an unscaled, or Doitsu, type of the Taisho Sanke variety.

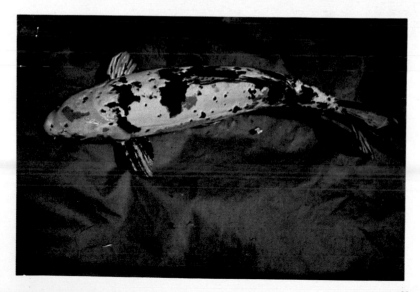

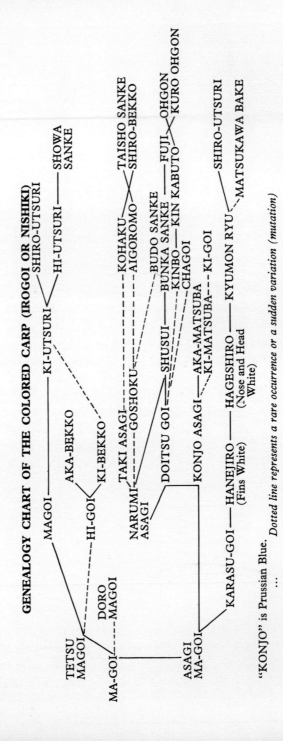

D. Discussion:

These three varieties may appear in the progeny from any of the other color varieties, but generally they come from the members of the Taisho-sanke and Kohaku varieties.

It would be impossible to select a show quality Bekko while it is young, because there is an inherent tendency to change color and pattern many, many times before maturity.

ASAGI

Asagi

A. Discussion: Asagi magoi is the first of a variety developed directly from the Ma-goi (probably a mutation).
B. Description: A koi with a blue or gray top half and red or orange fins, cheeks, and undersides. The Asagi may be either the Doitsu type or normally scaled type. The Doitsu type is called Shusui and was discussed earlier.
C. Selection hints:
   1. The red or orange color of the fins, cheeks, and undersides should be as dark, rich, and pure as possible.
   2. The blue or gray back color should be clear, with no blemishes of any other colors.
   3. The Gin-rei type of Asagi is very popular and in great demand. It is truly a gem of beauty and symmetry which will capture the hearts of many hobbyists who are fortunate enough to see a show specimen.

GOSHOKU

Goshoku (Five-colored koi; Goshiki)

A. Discussion: A good specimen of this color variety is the most highly prized of all in koi culture because it is a combination of five different colors united carefully and delicately into a pattern of perfection. The Japanese hobbyists say that a perfect specimen is like "a dainty cherry blossom in a forest of pines."

The Goshoku is said to be a mutation from the Narumi Asagi.
B. Description: Five-colored. The main color is generally dark (black or charcoal), with accents of red, brown, white, and blue or gray.

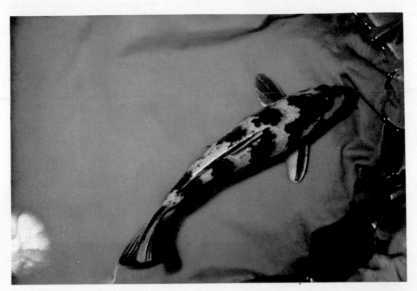

The Kin-ki-utsuri koi is very similar to the Ki-utsuri and Hi-Utsuri varieties but differs in being highly metallic.

The white coloration in the Shiro-utsuri should be evenly dispersed over the body, not localized in one or two major areas.

Hi-utsuri koi, but not a very good specimen.

The nicely symmetrical placement of the red and white color accents, coupled with the fish's good basic black body color, makes this a good specimen of the Showa-Sanke variety.

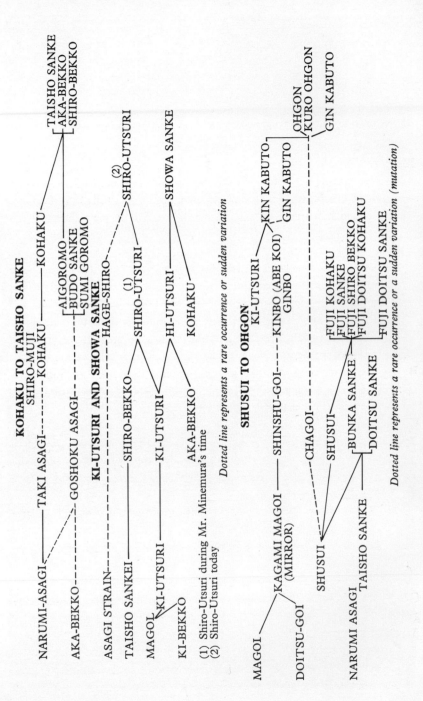

KOHAKU TO TAISHO SANKE

KI-UTSURI AND SHOWA SANKE

Dotted line represents a rare occurrence or sudden variation

(1) Shiro-Utsuri during Mr. Minemura's time
(2) Shiro-Utsuri today

SHUSUI TO OHGON

Dotted line represents a rare occurrence or a sudden variation (mutation)

C. Selection hints:

1. The exactness and uniformity of the pattern are the most important characters to consider in this variety, for the colors of the Goshoku may be masked and graded into light and dark shades on many parts of the body and finnage. However the complete pattern should be one of balance and unique quality.

BENI-KUJAKU
Kujaku (Peacock; Kin-sui; Kujaku-Ohgon)

A. Discussion: This variety is considered to be just a highly metallic colored Goshoku. As the name implies, it is multi-colored, like the peacock which it is said to resemble. It is a very recently developed variety, very pleasing to the eye, and is very popular in Hawaii at present.

Very little is known about how this variety was developed, but some hobbyists feel that it was created by breeding either the Asagi or the Shusui with the Nezumi-Ohgon.

Hobbyists who raise this color variety claim that it is one color variety that never loses its original colors in growth but instead becomes more beautiful as it matures.

B. Description: The term *Kujaku* means "peacock" in Japanese. The Kujaku is basically the same as the Goshoku, but it is highly metallic, like members of the Ohgon variety.

C. Selection hints:

1. The most important thing to consider when selecting a Kujaku is its metallic sheen, for the metallic sheen coupled with the five different colors is what gives this variety its unique and beautiful appearance.

2. This variety, like the other varieties, may be either of the Doitsu type or normally scaled.

3. All selection hints given in the Goshoku section also apply here.

KOHAKU GIN-LIN
Gin-Lin; Kin-Lin (phosphorescent silver; phosphorescent gold)

A. Description and Discussion: *Gin-Lin* in Japanese literally means "silver phosphorus" (*Gin* = silver; *Lin* = phosphorus), or phosphorescent silver. All the Gin-Lin type koi have highly phosphorescent silver specks on their scales. Any koi possessing this

Doitsu Ohgon; this specimen exhibits a good scale pattern along the lateral line, which is much desired in all Doitsu type koi.

Beni-Kujaku koi; note unblemished whiteness of the extended pectoral fin.

Poor specimen of the Ohgon variety.

Shiro-muji koi should be as completely monochromatic as possible.

The asymmetrical pattern of the lateral scalation of this Doitsu Sanke detracts from the value of the fish as a show specimen.

An albino koi showing the pink eyes characteristic of true albinos; albino koi bred to each other will breed true.

particular anatomical characteristic is classified as Gin-Lin. Those which have golden specks instead of silver specks on the scales are called "Kin-Lin." Therefore these Gin-Lin or Kin-Lin groups of koi should not be considered as separate color varieties but specific types of the different color varieties.

The specific types of Gin-Lin are as follows:

1. *Tsubu-Gin-Lin :* *Tsubu-Gin-Lin* in Japanese means "small specked with phosphorescent silver." In this type of Gin-Lin, the phosphorescent silver specks are scattered all over the top half of the koi's body, regardless of any design or pattern.

2. *Beta-Gin-Lin :* In this type of Gin-Lin, the silver specks are much larger than in the Tsubu type and are arranged in parallel lines over the top half of the koi's body.

3. *Gin-Rei :* This type is similar to the Gin-Lin except that the silver specks form a thin fringe on the edge of each scale, giving the Koi's body a lacy effect. This type is very popular in the Asagi variety.

   The Gin-Lin or Kin-Lin type characteristic may occur in any of the non-metallic color varieties.

B. Selection hints:

1. In regard to pattern, color or shape, all comments made in the previous sections remain the same for each non-metallic color variety.

2. The quantity and the arrangement of the Gin or Kin specks usually determines the value of the Gin-Lin or Kin-Lin type of koi. The more Gin or Kin specks on the scales of the koi and the more uniform the arrangement of specks, the higher the value of the specimen.

3. In judging a specimen of this type of koi, all other physical attributes are of secondary importance.

KAWARI-MONO

Kawari-mono (Literally ,"changeable")

A. Description: Included in this group are koi of the Kohaku, Bekko, and Sanke color varieties with a highly metallic color throughout the body. During show time this special type of Kohaku, Bekko, and Sanke are placed and judged in their own color class.

B. Discussion: Since this type of koi is forever changing color it would be very hard to get a true photograph.

This type of koi has many dedicated fanciers especially here in Hawaii, but a perfect specimen is almost impossible to obtain.

C. Selection hints:
   1. The highly metallic body color coupled with the other attributes cited in the sections on Kohaku, Bekko, and Sanke should be sought while making the selection.
   2. Personal tastes and desires should be the only guide to selection after the above basic attributes are considered.

HENGE (NEZUMI-OHGON)
Bake-mono or Henge (Literally ,"Ghost")

A. Description: The above terms are applied to koi which undergo seasonal color changes. For example: A change from black to black and white, then to all white; then back to complete black again.

B. Selection hints:
   1. All selection hints given in the previous sections on the particular color variety should be followed.
   2. No hard and fast rules should be followed in selecting a koi of this type because of its ever-changing color and pattern.
   3. Personal tastes and desires should be the guide to follow in selection.

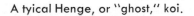

A tyical Henge, or "ghost," koi.

Although this is not a good specimen of the Shiro-muji type, it bears the highly metallic scales that are often found on Doitsu koi.

Shiro-Bekko koi showing the typical tortoise-shell pattern of this color variety.

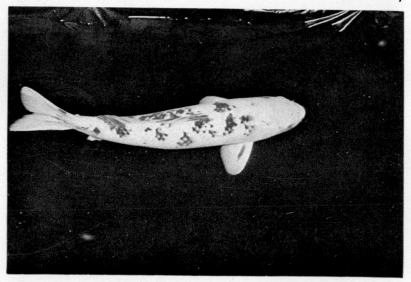

This dorsal view of an Asagi koi shows the variety's gray-blue back and the patches of orange and red on the rest of the body.

A representative five-colored koi known as the Showa variety.

Diseases and Treatments

There are many diseases of koi, but my discussion will be confined to the more common ones.

1. Anchor worms

The most aggravating disease condition experienced by most beginners is an infestation of anchor worms (*Lernaea carassi*). The anchor worm (a copepod) is a small external parasite which imbeds itself under the scales and skin of the koi. Here it stays and feeds until it lays eggs to begin a new cycle. This parasite is a quarter to half an inch in length when mature and is capable of causing a large welt or raw area where it is imbedded. The real threat to the fish is not actually the anchor worm itself but the establishment of a passage way for a secondary infection to enter.

Prescribed treatment: A 5% solution of potassium permanganate was the standard treatment before, but it has now been replaced by an aquatic insecticide which has been developed in Japan. The trade name of this aquatic insecticide, made by the Bayer Co., is "Dipterex." Care should be undertaken when using this insecticide, for it is very toxic. The prescribed dosage is one capful (1 c.c.) per 360–400 gals. of water to be treated. Treated water need not be replaced by fresh water (as must be done in the potassium permanganate treatment.)

Dipterex remains active only for one day, so the pond water should be treated every four days for a period of two weeks to insure complete treatment. As a preventive measure, Dipterex may be added at the same concentration (1 cap per 360–400 gals. of water) every seven days.

A koi with a crooked spine is the result of an overdose of Dipterex— if the overdose did not kill the koi. Despite the few years that this product has been on the market, the author has seen many such specimens. Misuse of this product is the only reason for such an occurrence.

If potassium permanganate treatment is preferred, you may acquire a commercial preparation. The treatment procedure found on the package should be used. The author has seen many catastrophes caused by an overdose and misuse of potassium permanganate, so be very careful.

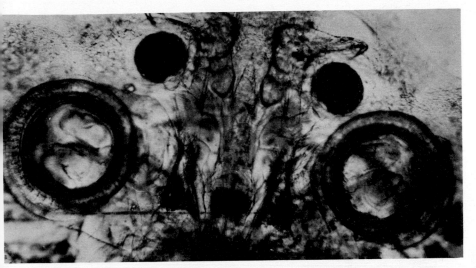

Closeup of the head of a fish louse, giving a very good view of the mouth parts.

2. Fish Lice (*Argulus foliaceus*)

The fish louse is another common parasite found in koi ponds. This too is now being controlled by careful use of Dipterex.

The fish louse, a copepod, is a flat animal measuring about $\frac{1}{4}$ inch long by $\frac{1}{8}$ inch wide which swims free in the water. It attaches itself to the fish and sucks its blood, causing inflammation and anemia. Koi affected by this parasite will gather in a corner. They suffer from anemic languor and will show less and less appetite for food; if left untreated, they ultimately will die.

Since the parasite cannot be easily detected by amateurs, it is essential to use a drug whenever the disease is suspected.

Remedy

Dipterex-conc. 1/150,000,000. While the adult parasite can be killed within 10 hours in this manner, the eggs may not be completely destroyed. It is therefore desirable to follow this procedure every two months. Even when there is no evidence of the parasite it is a good practice to employ the drug every four to five months.

3. Bacterial and Fungal Diseases

Bacterial and fungal diseases may be controlled very satisfactorily by commercially available preparations containing malachite green, a dye that possesses both bactericidal and fungicidal properties.

The pure white pectoral fins of this representative of the Kawari-Mono type contrast nicely with the bright orange color of its head.

The phosphorescent specklings of the Kohaku Gin-Lin give this koi variety an interesting iridescent appearance. Photo by the author.

This traditional goldfish pond would serve equally well as a comfortable home for koi.

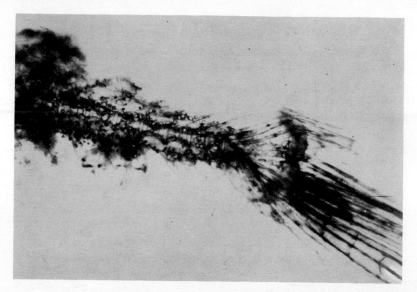

Closeup of the tail of a fish badly infected by tail rot.

If a malachite green-base preparation fails to give satisfactory results, try antibiotic treatment using a broad-spectrum, inexpensive antibiotic such as poultry grade Aureomycin. Terramycin, Achromycin V and Streptomycin may also be used. The prescribed dosage of the above mentioned antibiotics is generally 250 mg.–500 mg. per 5 liters of water. Since treating a large pond with these antibiotics will be very expensive, antibiotic treatment should be undertaken in a small container.

When treating koi with any of the above medicants, all filtration should be stopped, but strong aeration should be maintained. Acriflavine immersion is also very good for bacterial and fungal diseases if other treatments fail. Treatment consists of placing the diseased koi in an Acriflavine solution of a concentration of 1 gm. of Acriflavine per 100 liters of water for two to three days. Since plants are affected by the Acriflavine, treatment should be undertaken in a plant-free container.

4. Scrapes, cuts and bruises

Treat scrapes, cuts and bruises of koi by swabbing the damaged area with ordinary household 2% Mercurochrome solution. The koi should be netted daily and the treatment repeated until the damaged area is healed. This treatment is inexpensive and very effective.

TREATMENTS

Since treatment techniques differ from place to place, the following section is a summary of treatments and diseases found in Japan. I am including them here because Japanese koi fanciers have had a great deal of experience with their fish, and experience-proved results are well worth passing on.

I. Drugs used
Concentration used

1. Dipterex (aquatic insecticide—an organic phosphonate) 0.25–0.33 ppm.
2. Dyes:
   (*a*) Acriflavine (neutral)—use just enough to tint the pond water green
   (*b*) Malachite green 1/500,000
3. Aureomycin (aqueous solution) 1 gm. aureomycin to 32 gals. of pond water
4. Others:
   (*a*) Potassium permanganate
   (*b*) Ointments:
      1. Penicillin
      2. Chloromycetin
   (*c*) Aqueous solution as topical applicant
      1. Mercurochrome 2%
5. Other antibiotics used:
   (*a*) Achromycin

II. Diseases
1. MATSUKASA DISEASE
   (*a*) *Discussion:* "Probably" the same disease as what we know as dropsy.
   (*b*) *Symptoms:* Swelling of the body resulting in the protrusion of the scales of affected koi. The body closely resembles a pine cone (the Japanese word for pine cone is *Matsukasa*). There is a loss of equilibrium, and the diseased fish tends to float to the surface.
   (*c*) *Treatment:* Isolate the affected fish as soon as possible. Clean the pond immediately and treat with an aqueous solution of either Aureomycin or Achromycin at prescribed dosage.

The fish at left is a representative of the Asagi variety.

1. Kohaku
2. Harewake-Ohgon
3. Taisho-Sanke
4. Ki-goi
5. Shiro-utsuri
6. Hi-utsuri
7. Kin-kabuto (?)
8. Shusui
9. Kin-Ki-utsuri
10. Ki-utsuri
11. Showa-Sanke
12. Aka-muji
13. Shiro-Bekko
14. Kohaku (Gin-goke)
15. Shiro-muji
16. Taki-Asagi
17. Orange-Ohgon
18. Gin-Kabuto (?)
19. Karasu-goi

Japanese fanciers feel that most koi will recover if the disease is treated early enough. (*Note:* If this is dropsy, there is no known cure, but antibiotic therapy sometimes helps.)

COMMON COLD DISEASE

(*a*) *Discussion:* Symptoms are very similar to what aquarists call "Ich," but may be a little different in character.

(*b*) *Symptoms:* Foggy white dots appear on the koi's skin. This symptom may be caused by an abrupt drop in water temperature.

(*c*) *Treatment:* Readjust water temperature as soon as possible. The koi should respond to this treatment in four to five days. If complications arise, the koi should be treated immediately with an antibiotic such as Aureomycin, etc., to prevent any secondary problems.

3. HAKUTEN DISEASE (*Ichthyophthirius*)

(*a*) This is the "Ich" or "Ick" or "white spot" disease familiar to tropical fish hobbyists.

(*b*) *Symptoms:* Small white spots appear on the fins and body of the koi. The koi becomes sluggish, loses its appetite, and will scrape itself periodically to try to rid itself of the parasites causing the condition.

The ciliated protozoan *Ichthyophthirius multifilis*, parasite cause of the disease "Ich."

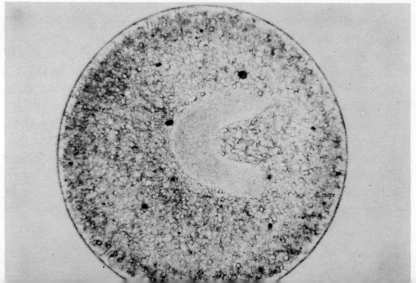

(c) *Treatment:* Japanese hobbyists recommend a treatment with either quinine sulfate or Dipterex. Cure is obtained in six to seven days in moderate water temperatures but will take about 13 days if the water temperature is lower. Acriflavine immersion and treatment with quinine hydrochloride (1 gram of quinine hydrochloride per 100–150 liters of water) are also very effective and economical treatments, as are a number of the commercial aquarium remedies on the market.

Ich, caused by the protozoan organism *Ichthyophthirius multifilis,* is a comparatively common disease of captive fishes, especially tropical fishes, but Ich will seldom attack healthy mature koi. It is only when koi are kept under very unsanitary conditions that the koi will become enfeebled enough for the parasite to get a foothold. Young koi maintained under unfavorable conditions are much more likely than adult koi to become infested; unfortunately, it is with the young fish that Ich has the greatest potential for damage.

4. OKUSARE DISEASE
   (a) *Discussion:* This disease is probably what English-speaking aquarists call fin and tail rot. If it is fin and tail rot, the disease is caused by a bacterium and therefore should respond nicely to any type of bactericidal treatment.
   (b) *Symptoms:* The tail and fins of the koi become a foggy white. This discoloration will then spread to other parts of the koi's body, affecting the koi by making it very sick and weak.

5. DOROKABURI DISEASE
   (a) *Symptom:* When viewed from above, the sides of the koi appear to be covered with mud. This condition is the result of a fatty diet.
   (b) *Treatment:* Place the koi on a fat-free diet. The koi should start to respond after a few days of this diet treatment.

6. FUNGAL DISEASES
   (a) *Symptoms:* Cottony-like material on the koi in areas which have been in some way diseased or damaged. The fungus may take a hold on any part of the body without any preference for any particular area.

(b) *Treatment*: Immerse the affected koi in a solution containing a combination of Dipterex and malachite green (conc. 1/500,000,000) or Dipterex and Acriflavine neutral.

7. INTESTINAL INFLAMMATION

(a) *Symptoms*: Bloody pus in feces, constipation, sluggishness and loss of appetite. Blistering of the external wall of the intestines and exuding of a very viscous fluid are other symptoms. These symptoms are caused by a congested intestinal tract.

(b) *Treatment*: Only fresh natural foods that are easily digested should be fed to koi with such a condition. This diet should be continued until the intestinal inflammation subsides.

Stale foods should not be fed to the koi at any time, because such foods are a prime cause of intestinal inflammation.

8. EXTERNAL SCRAPES, CUTS, AND INJURIES

(a) *Symptoms*: Swelling, weeping, bleeding, and localized congestion in the injured area.

(b) *Treatment*: Injured area should be cleansed carefully with a diluted disinfectant to remove any foreign material in or around the injury. Next apply an antibiotic ointment such as penicillin and chloromycetin ointments to the injured area. This application of the ointment should be done at least two to three times a day until the injured area is healed. This topical application of antibiotic ointments will prevent suppuration and help hasten the healing process.

There are some diseases in koi culture which are often seen by many hobbyists but about which not much is known. I would like to mention just a few of these and express my opinion on them.

Hollow-back condition in koi

This condition is seen quite often in newly imported koi. The symptom consists of the degeneration of the muscles in the back area of the koi, resulting in a depressed area in this location. If the koi is viewed from the top, this hollow-back condition would make the koi look as if it had a very large head and a proportionately small and skinny body. This may be a secondary effect of a poor unbalanced diet or a form of cold water tuberculosis of koi. Many koi raisers believe that very cold water conditions cause this symptom, but no dependable data or explanation on this symptom is presently available.

A beautiful collection of koi in a Japanese koi pond landscaped in the traditional fashion.

Stunting, pop-eye, parrot-mouth condition of highly metallic koi progeny
A combination of the above-mentioned symptoms can be seen in the progeny of a breeding between two highly metallic parents. The author and many other koi raisers feel that these symptoms are not the result of any disease, but a genetic defect or aberration of some sort. The association of these symptoms with the extra highly metallic colored progeny suggests strongly that this highly metallic color character somehow expresses a "genetic weakness" which manifests itself in these undesirable characters. Since not enough data is available on this subject, it is up to the individual hobbyist to select the breeder koi to prevent the condition from occurring in their own spawnings. A suggestion would be to avoid breeding very highly colored metallic individuals. Good results will depend on many trial and error matings and much experimentation. As in anything else there may be individual koi which are exceptions to the rule, and these must be handled accordingly.

93

"Whirling" disease in young koi

This condition may be recognized by the "whirling" or "spiraling" swimming motion of the affected koi. This symptom is seen only when the koi are in the active process of swimming. At rest, the diseased koi look very much normal. But as the disease progresses, the young koi are not able to maintain themselves in their characteristic position.

This disease is caused by a parasitic protozoan, *Lentospora cerebalis*. These protozoans bore through the cartilage of the skull and destroy the balancing center of the brain.

Treatment for this disease is unknown. The best thing to do is to destroy all koi which are affected in this way.

The cause of this disease is poor maintenance of the fry rearing ponds, i.e., over-crowding, over-feeding, and use of uncleansed tubifex worms.

After all the affected koi are destroyed and the rearing ponds thoroughly cleaned, treat the ponds with a commercial sterilizing agent and crude salt (about 1 tablespoon per gallon of water). Make sure the pond is flushed thoroughly before fish are re-introduced. Since this disease is not very virulent, if these steps are taken immediately, it can easily be controlled before it gets out of hand.

Distorted body shape of the different Ohgon varieties

The symptom is a distorted bloated body shape of the koi (generally of the Ohgon variety).

This condition is not a disease, but probably an inherited anatomical character of the Ohgon varieties. Because of the distorted body shape of these koi, detrimental factors such as over-feeding, lack of exercise, and egg-binding in females may intensify the condition.

The only thing a hobbyist can do to keep Ohgon koi from getting into this condition is to watch the diet carefully and provide more exercise for them. Since it is not a disease, one should not be alarmed by its appearance in his collection.

Preventive procedure is the only control here if you wish to have a collection which is in every way aesthetically pleasing.

The hobbyist also must learn to tell the difference between a roe-laden female and one with the above-mentioned condition. Only practice can teach you to do this accurately.

Loss of color in koi

This condition is thought by many authorities to be definitely a diet deficiency problem, but there are no dependable data to support this. "Water chemistry" has been also blamed as another probable cause of the loss in color but, here too, data are not available to support the theory. At the moment, no one knows for certain what causes koi to lose color.

Miscellaneous

Cosmetic surgery of koi

Since the trend in koi culture in the past few years has been toward a very high caliber of work, the result has been an emphasis of show quality koi instead of mediocre specimens. Because of this, the practice of cosmetic surgery on koi has been developed.

Cosmetic surgery is confined to the removal of pigmented tissue, blemishes, and scales on show quality koi so that the specimen will remain acceptable for show.

The procedure practiced is as follows:

1. Carefully catch the koi that needs surgery.
2. Place the fish in a shallow pan or bucket containing a fish tranquilizer.
3. Hold koi steady with the help of a friend. With a tweezer or surgical scissors, remove the unwanted tissue, blemish, or scale carefully.
4. Paint the affected area with household 2% Mercurochrome solution daily to prevent an occurrence of a secondary infection. This cautionary step is very, very important, for a fish will be scarred for life if an infection results, thereby ending any possibility of showing it in the future.

This type of surgery might seem cruel and unnecessary to many of us, but nevertheless it is still carried on by the more serious koi fanciers who strive ceaselessly to attain perfection in their collections.

Transporting koi

Transporting koi is most easily done in very large plastic bags or containers which can be filled with a little water and a great amount of oxygen. These plastic containers are then placed in cardboard boxes to further support them for the trip.

A fish tranquilizer may be added to the water.

Conversion Table of Measures to aid in making up the medicants

FLUID MEASURES

1 drop (eye dropper) = 1/160 fluid oz. = 1/20 c.c. (or ml.).

1 teaspoon = $\frac{1}{8}$ fluid oz. = 4 c.c.

1 tablespoon = 2/3 fluid oz. = 20 c.c.

1 ml. (Milliliter) = 1 c.c. (cubic centimeter) = 0.001 liter.

1 gal. (U.S.) = 3.7853 liters = 3,785.4 c.c. = 4 quarts = 128 fluid ounces.

1 pint (U.S.) = 0.473 liter = 473.179 c.c. = 16 fluid ounces.

1 quart (U.S.) = 0.946 liter = 946.358 c.c. = 32 fluid ounces.

1 teacup = 6 fluid oz. = 180 c.c.

SOLID MEASURES

1 mg. (milligram) = 0.015 grain = 0.001 gram.

1 gm. (gram) = 15.4324 grains = 0.0022 pound (avoirdupois) = 1000 mg.

1 pound = 16 ounces (avoirdupois) = 7000 grains = 453.59 grams.

1 level teaspoon = 75 grains = 5 grams.

1 level tablespoon = 300 grains = 20 grams.

1 teacup = 7 oz. = 220 grams.

1 ppm. = 1 mg./liter or 1 mg./1000 ml.

REFERENCES

BROCK, VERNON E.: The Introduction of Aquatic Animals into Hawaiian Waters. Pg. 469.

HIROOKA, HYOHEI: The Care and Training of Koi. March 20, 1964.

MAKINO, S.: The Chromosomes of the Carp, Cyprinus carpio, including those of some related Species of Cyrinidae for comparison Cytologia, Vol. 9, No. 4, 1939.

MAKINO, S.: A Karyological Study of Goldfish of Japan, Ibid. Vol. 12, No. 1, 1941.

MAKINO, S., Y. OJIMA and Y. MATSUI: Some Cytological Features of Sterility in the Carp-funa Hybrids. Annot. Zool. Japonensis. Vo. 128, No. 1, 1955.

MAKINO, S., Y. OJIMA and Y. MATSUI: Cytogenetical and Cytochemical Studies in Carp-funa Hybrids. The Nucleus, Vol. 1, No. 2, 1958.

MATSUI, Y.: Genetical studies of Fresh Water Fish II. On the Hybrid of Cyprinus carpio L. and Carassius carassius (L.). Journ. Imp. Fisheries Experimental Station Tokyo, No. 2, 1931.

MATSUI, Y.: Genetical Studies on Fresh Water Fish III. On the Male Sterility of Hybrids of Cyprinus carpio L. and Carassius carassius (L.) or its Varieties. Ibid. No. 3, 1933.

MATSUI, Y. and S. MAKINO: On Intersexuality in the Carp-funa hybrids. Zoological Magazine (Tokyo) Vol. 47, 1935 (in Japanese).

SEELEY, H. G. (F.R.S.): Cyprinus carpio (Linnaeus)—The Carp. The Fresh-Water Fishes of Europe. Pg. 94–104.